DREAM

DREAM

GREAT SECRETS ARE REVEALED IN YOUR DREAMS

REV. DR. MATTHEW OGBONMWAN

iUniverse, Inc.
Bloomington

DREAM
Great Secrets Are Revealed in Your Dreams

iUniverse books may be ordered through booksellers or by contacting:

iUniverse
1663 Liberty Drive
Bloomington, IN 47403
www.iuniverse.com
1-800-Authors (1-800-288-4677)

ISBN: 978-1-4759-6524-7 (sc)
ISBN: 978-1-4759-6526-1 (hc)
ISBN: 978-1-4759-6525-4 (ebk)

Library of Congress Control Number: 2012923336

Printed in the United States of America

iUniverse rev. date: 12/19/2012

CONTENTS

Dedication ix

Special Thanks xi

Preface.. xiii

Foreword... xvii

Introduction... xxi

Chapter One

The Different Ways Of Communicating With God........................1

    Vision is one of the ways God speaks to us.....................3

    The record of vision in the Old Testament 4

    The record of vision in the New Testament....................5

    Urim And Thummim were forms of

    communication in the Old Testament 6

    The Record of Prophetic Utterances in the Old

    And New Testaments...7

Chapter Two

How You Hear From God Through Dream 11

    God still speaks through Dream..................................11

    Vital and foundational facts about dreams 12

    The role of the Holy Spirit in the fulfillment

    of your Dream 14

Chapter Three

Your Future And Salvation Are Revealed In Your Dream............19

There are several occurrences where God
communicated with Joseph.......................................20

The two dreams of Joseph are unfolded
(gen. 37:5-9)..20

The second Dream strengthened Joseph.......................22

Joseph's Dreams were used as protective
and Guiding Gyrus...25

The wise men went to search for the new born 29

Dreams direct, guide and protect the dreamer..............30

Chapter Four

Dreams Provide Needed Clues For Crucial Decisions.................33

Jesus was accused before Pontius Pilate....................35

Pilate's wife had a warning dream from God 36

God spoke to King Nebuchadnezzar through
a dream..37

The anxiety of a king who forgot his dream 39

Chapter Five

*Looking At Hindrances, Trials, And Temptations
In The Life Of A Chosen Vessel* 41

Potiphar's wife falsely accused Joseph 43

Those you help may forget you 45

You have a role in fulfilling your dream..................47

Chapter Six

The Leadership And Provision Of God

In The Fulfillment Of Your Dream 49

(A) God's favor is available upon your life 49

(B) Gift of Interpretation is available............................50

(C) God gives the gift of Knowledge 52

(D) Apostle James reminds us that God

gives wisdom to any one who asks 52

Your dreams will come true...53

There are stages of the manifestation

of your dream 55

Jacob went to Egypt as directed by Dream 56

The Land of Goshen represents

Dream Come True..57

Goshen is your destination...58

Chapter Seven

God And His Word Are One..63

I wish to offer my concluding statements 64

About The Author...69

Cast For The Book "Dream" 71

DEDICATION

To all my beloved who seek to know, hear and obey God. To all who know their callings but seek to clearly understand their pathway to Godliness and their direction for fulfillment of God's calling.

SPECIAL THANKS

To Pastor Betty Asemota, the executive secretary of Christ Apostolic Church of God Mission Overseas Parish, who spent hours typing and editing this manuscript. Her tenacity and dedication helped me to focus and get this book out despite my heavy travelling schedule.

May God bless her and all her loved ones in Jesus, name.

I wish to use this medium to express my unreserved appreciation to her Excellency, Bishop Diana Adjartey, president of GPN Worldwide, who shared vital information, counseled and prayed during the production of this book. I am grateful to her husband, Rev. Dr. Francis and their wonderful children.

Finally, there are many known and unknown loved ones who keep me in their fervent prayers, and reach out to me in this Missionary journey, to those I say, God bless you. My wonderful wife, Rev. Bernel, children, grand-children, Josiah (the newly born Grand baby Oct.17,2012) and Members of CACGM Worldwide, you are blessed and favored by God.

PREFACE

Every child of God is with a designed blue print for his or her life. Many spend their lifetime attempting to discover that particular designed life blue print for navigating and succeeding in life.

Some people discover the blue print half way along their life span, and once they discovered they start the building plan for their life. They may finally succeed with much and tougher endeavor before death do them part. A good example of this was Apostle Paul on his road to Damascus. He spent a major part of his life breathing and slaughtering the disciples of the Lord Jesus, whom he finally defended. He became apologetic all his life time after finding his purpose for life through revelation. He propagated the Gospel of Jesus through his preaching, teaching, and literature than any of the Disciples as recorded in the New Testament.

On the other hand, some go through life groping, getting frustrated and wondering where they missed it in life. As a result of this frustration, they cultivate some habits, practices and such activities like Jacob in the bible. Jacob stole his brother's birthright. Another example is Simon in the scripture who offered money to the Apostle hoping by so doing people will receive the Holy Ghost when he lays hands on them.

The third class of people received the blue print fully or partially at their early stages of life. I called these the blessed people because they paid attention to their dreams and sought the interpretation. They received instructions that guide them through this rough journey of the Earth. A very good example of this category is my main Character, Joseph, who is the focus of this book.

The revelation of God's plan (I call it blue print) aided him to be focused, determined, kept him from horrendous sins and guided him to keep his mind on God. In many circumstances that would have caused many to lose faith, trust and dependence on God Joseph on the other hand held to God.

He believed that God, who has begun a good work in him will complete it. When the Butler forgot him in jail, he did not become bitter, but trusted. God for his dreams.

This book is not about interpretations of dreams, visions nor other forms through which God speaks, but it to challenge the readers to seek your specific (purpose) blue print. It is not anything to disregard, nor be ignorant of. The Lord said "my people perish for the lack of knowledge" God does not make anything without a purpose and his purpose for one's life is the blue print that we must seek in our lives. Jesus himself said that his meat is to do the work of his father, God. The scripture further emphasizes this statement by saying "for the purpose was the son of man manifested".

Modeica, in the Old Testament reminded Queen Esther to seek for God's blue print for her life; perhaps it is for this purpose (task at hand) God raised her. Esther, an orphan and a foreigner, was chosen as the wife of the King. It was only the king who had the authority to change the decree against the Jews. This reminder challenged Queen Esther to declare a fast to enable her discover her Purpose (Dream) for life. The purpose of your life is hidden in your dream, and the understanding of it brings fulfillment and success.

Matthew Ogbonmwan

FOREWORD

What a joy to know when God speaks to you and you are very sure you heard from him and no one else! How distinctive can this be? In fact, this book does not tell you that this is how God speaks, but, takes you through a journey that enables you come to a convincing conclusion, where you finally declare within you that certainly this is God, "He has spoken to me".

There are times when you read a book usually it is expected that the title addresses certain burning questions in your mind hence you picked it off the shelf of the bookstore. Well, while reading the book, interesting it may seem, you realize that it has not addressed these questions.

However, "Dream" enables you to ask and answer questions pertaining to your ability to seek clear understanding and direction for God's calling upon your life. I often ask myself, how will I know what God has spoken concerning a particular area or aspect or situation of my life? In this book, the author skillfully peels the onion bulb, layer by layer exposing its core to the reader enabling us to continue to dream by taking a closer look at those before us that dreamed and what became of them, their dreams and how those dreams are still being fulfilled to this day.

These pages are not only about stories of dreamers and their dreams but situations that culminates the past and the present, in the sense that we might think that God only revealed himself to the people and prophets of old a certain way, and no longer operates that way. For example, the way God revealed to Joseph his future, through series of dreams, navigated the heart, home and security of Joseph and Mary through series dreams. That same God desires to do same today in our lives if we allow him by being humble, obedient, forgiving and trusting our lives into his hands, in Jesus name, Amen.

If you have never met the author of this book, I'll say that you have just met him through his writing. He writes the way he speaks, filled with God's anointing, humor and a heart for the children of God. Rev. Dr. Matthew Ogbonmwan is the foreign Mission Superintendent of the overseas Parish of Christ Apostolic Church of God Mission (CACGM). For years he has led people to experience God's presence through conventions, conferences, crusades in most parts of Europe, Africa and some parts of the United Sates of America. He is a church planter, he believes in the expansion of the gospel of our Lord and savior Jesus Christ. He is a family man and lives with his lovely wife of over thirty 30 years, children and grand children in Houston Texas.

In closing, I'll like to say that in as much as I do not know what areas you are seeking God's divine revelation, as you read "Dream" your spirit will be lifted up to pray because there are powerful prayers within that you cannot but shout a loud Hallelujah or a loud Amen as is stirred up within you. You will be filled with the Holy Spirit of Revival. How resourceful and refreshing! Your life will never be the same again.

-EMSO B. ASEMOTA
Pastor, Christ Apostolic Church
of God Mission Int., Bronx Branch
Executive Secretary, Overseas Foreign Mission

Introduction

A little literature review on the ways God talks to his children, I thought would suffice before I zero in on my topic—Dream. Little did I know that my review would take me months and volumes of pages to the extent that got me lost in a journey that will take months to retrieve my steps.

Well, if my schedule will permit me that will not be a bad journey. Many religious leaders have told us that they heard specifically from God. Some of these leaders or religious groups include Mormons, Christians' science, Jehovah witness, Seventh day Adventist. Dr. Martin Luther King Jr., and many others political and civil rights activists have their version of hearing from God.

In the Bible, Apostle Paul's motivation was centered upon the voice of Jesus, the Son of God, (vision) on the Damascus road. Great men and women past and present take time to hear from their maker, the one who designed and planned their lives.

There are very many ways God speaks to people, and it is needful to mention some before I concentrate on my area of interest. I looked at several scriptures, literatures, folklores, myths, but for me and my readers' safety, I choose to utilize the Holy Bible as the inspired word of God. II Timothy 3:16, "All scripture is given by inspiration of God, and is profitable for doctrine, for reproof, for correction, for instruction, in righteousness: That the man of God may be perfect, thoroughly furnished unto all good works (KJV)." My goal is not here to prove the validity of the Bible as the inspired word of God. I believe this is already settled with those who profess their faith in Jesus Christ.

We can find many methods of revelation or communication for direction from God in the Bible. So let us navigate some of these ways in the following pages.

I believe that this journey with me will be worth the effort. I urge you to read this book prayerfully and ask the Holy Spirit to minister to you.

CHAPTER ONE

THE DIFFERENT WAYS OF COMMUNICATING WITH GOD

I Samuel 28:6 - When Saul saw the Philistine camp, he
was afraid and trembled violently. He inquired of the
Lord, but the Lord did not answer him in <u>dreams</u> or by
<u>Urim </u>or by the prophets. Saul then said to his servants
"find me a woman who is a medium, so I can go and
consult her".

Saul was the man in Israel that God had instructed Prophet Samuel
to anoint as the king over his people. The Israelites were specially
delivered from bondage, and it is required that they follow the
divine direction of God. Initially, God was pleased with King
Saul, and he rose to a position of honor and he glorified God.
There was Joy and peace in Israel and the neighboring Nations
feared Israel as a Nation. The direction of God brings fullness of
joy. It is God's desire for his children to hear from him regularly.
Adam heard from God in the Garden of Eden regularly. In short,
Yahweh visited and communicated with him daily. There is
direction in one's life that requires regular instruction and not
only during crisis. Do not wait for instance of crisis before you

1

hear from your maker. After King Saul repeatedly disobeyed God, he was hiding and denied his daily guidance from God. He felt alienated from his source of direction; he forgot his God and depended on his human resources which failed him woefully when the Philistine camped in his territory. He did not even know until the enemies surrounded him. Psalm 91:1(KJV), "the one who lives under the protection of God, dwells in the shadow of the Almighty!"

He was afraid and troubled violently! He did what normal person would do. He sought direction from God through three means of the sources of direction and communication.

Unfortunately, the Lord we are told did not communicate through any of these means. Out of frustration, King Saul, went seeking after familiar spirit. Needless to say this is demon tactics, peeping devices contrary to God's divine communication. We must hear from God and that is why I started earlier that it is exasperating and frustrating to be void of direction.

Today, even some Christians, sad to say, go seeking for familiar spirit, medium, divinations, enchantments, palm readers and soothsayers to hear from Heaven. God is not dead and he spoke before and still speaks today. Heb.13:8 states that Jesus Christ is the same yesterday, today, and forever.

VISION IS ONE OF THE WAYS GOD SPEAKS TO US

Definitions:

The word Vision first occurred in Genesis 15:1. Apparently, it seems God was still speaking directly with human and may be still physically visiting human being. In Genesis chapter one through three, God was visiting and conversing with man. In Genesis chapter four, verse four through five; Abel presented his offering to God as well as Cain. God also asked Cain why he was furious and finally God told Cain his brother's blood cries out to him (God). Throughout the chapter God facially communicated with man. I know you would love to do so today. Won't you? Remember also in chapter seven the Lord told Noah to undergo a superfluous task of camping in the Ark for a long period of time. I know alright that it has to take face to face talk with God to accommodate all types of animals. By the way how did the animals get along with each other? There are bunch of questions to be answered but not in this book. God Bless you.

Chapter eleven gives account of the visitation of God to the Towel of Babel. Quickly, the earth exploded with a lot of people. The sons of God, (Fallen Angels?), came and got human beings pregnant thereby resulting in ruthless children. The earth got messed up with all types of people, Homosexuals, lesbians, deceivers, killers, and all vices and atrocities. In chapter twelve,

God still managed to call Abram and promised him blessings. "Now the Lord had said unto Abram, Get thee out of thy country . . . . that I will show you. In Genesis chapter twelve Verse four, Abram departed as the Lord had spoken unto him. Let us state what the Bible says, "As the Lord had spoken to him". Now in Genesis chapter fifteen verse one, we read that after these things the word of the Lord came to Abram in a vision: The vision records a long conversation between both. Vision can occur in the night or day. This is not a dream but communication with absence of sleep.

There are several other places in the old and New Testaments we see this word (vision) mentioned.

THE RECORD OF VISION IN THE OLD TESTAMENT

- Genesis 46:2 - That night, God spoke to Israel in a vision.
- Ezekiel 1:1- Ezekiel grew up in Jerusalem and most of his writings are visions. He received a variety of unusual visions concerning immediate and long-term plans of God.
- Joel 2 - The book of Joel foretells of God pouring out his Spirit upon all flesh, which will lead to sons and

daughter prophesying, old men dreaming dreams and young men seeing vision.

☞ Job 4:13 ~ Old Job, the man who desired to hear from God desperately spoke of visions of the nights.

THE RECORD OF VISION IN THE NEW TESTAMENT

a) Acts 9:10 ~ "Ananias was instructed in a vision to go to the street called straight where brother Saul is praying for God's direction.

b) Acts 16:6-10 ~ Here, Apostle Paul during his Europe Evangelization was instructed and directed in a vision to proceed to Macedonian.

c) Other references include:

1. Acts 22:17-18,

2. Acts 23:11,

3. 2 Corinth. 12:1-4,

4. Rev. 1:12-16

URIM AND THUMMIM WERE FORMS OF COMMUNICATION IN THE OLD TESTAMENT

Definition:

(a)   In Ezra 2:63, the Urim and Thummim were strong methods of communicating and hearing from God. Some tribes of Israelites (priesthood) were banned from participating in the feast of Holy Meal until the other priests consulted the Urim and Thummim.

(b)   The book of Ezra was written between 457 and 444 B.C. I understand from Literature review that this era coincided with the period of Guatam Budha in Indian, Confucius in China, Socrates of Greece and Pericles in Athens. This was after the exile and the temple was destroyed and many prophets and Israelites could not sing the Lord's songs while in exile. So the use of Urim & Thummim became popular.

(c) Exodus 28:30 - Aaron was instructed to enter the sanctuary placing the Urim & Thummim in the breast-plate for decisions.

(d) There are other passages you could read, and these include:

  1 Leviticus 8:8;

  2 Numbers 27:21;

  3 Deuteronomy 33:8,

  4 I Samuel 23: 9 (Ephod)

  5 I Samuel 30:7

  6 Nehemiah 7:65

  7 Judges 1:1; Judges 20:18

  8 Numbers 28:26

THE RECORD OF PROPHETIC UTTERANCES IN THE OLD AND NEW TESTAMENTS

Information:

This is the Era of the Prophets of God. It is interesting to know that Samuel was the last judge and first prophet of God as recorded in the book of Samuel. Prophets speak without fear or favor and many suffered for their activities. All through the Old testaments starting from the book of Samuel, God spoke, and directed the affairs of the nation, through the Prophets. There are two categories of prophets namely, minor and major prophets. The one clarified as minor, for example, Ezra, Haggai, Hosea and Joel were not less used but either their time space was shorter or the data on them were not much. The Major Prophets like Samuel, Elisha, Elijah, Ezekiel, Jeremiah and etc. were avenue of instructions, warnings, directions, from God. Mentions were equally made of prophetic activities in the New Testament. Luke 1:6, refers to a child who shall be called the Prophet of the Highest, referring to John the Baptist.

Acts 3:22 "for Moses truly said unto the fathers. A prophet shall the Lord your God raise up unto you of your brethren. Like unto me, him shall ye hear in all things whatsoever he shall say unto you". Acts 21:9-11, narrates the story of an Evangelist with four daughters, who were virgins, and did prophesy; they prophesied that danger awaited Apostle Paul. In verse 11, when Paul came to the people, Prophet Agabus, prophetically told him, he would be bound by Jews in Jerusalem.

Other means include the following:

a) Divine Revelation
b) Revelation through the Holy Spirit (Acts 5)
c) Christ Revelation as in book of Revelation through John
d) Fuller Revelation -Natural surrounding and circum- stances

e)   By Rhema Logos (Word of God, the Epistle)

f)   Trials and birth (Gen. 32:22-32)

g)   Audible voice (Job 33:16)

h)   Personal Appearance ~face to face Num. 12:7; Gen. 32:30

i)   Acts of God ~ Gen. 7:17, Gen. 8

j)   This, DREAM, is my area of focus which I believe God will help us to explain as it is very vital in this dispensation.

CHAPTER TWO

HOW YOU HEAR FROM GOD
THROUGH DREAM

There are various ways today by prayer, fasting, and reading the scriptures that enable you through dreams hear from God.

GOD STILL SPEAKS THROUGH DREAM

The Bible, as well as other scriptures or great books of historical and revealed religion, show traces of beliefs in dreams. Christians assign a very important attention to bible-aligned dreams, and other religions do also. There are logical reasons for accepting information conveyed in dreams, in as much as narratives in the Bible speak of divine guidance by this means. God clearly stated that He would speak through dreams and visions in the Old Testament.

> "He said, listen to my words: when prophets are among you, I, the Lord will show myself to them in visions; I will speak to them in visions; I will speak to them in dreams" (Numbers 12:6 KJV).

The Bible records many occasions of dreams as super natural revelation sent from God to direct, warn, instruct, show, correct, and confirm his words. God uses dreams also to prove and validate his true servants; for example, Pontius Pilate's wife as we will disclose later in this Book. Moreover, there are some servants of God endowed with the knowledge and wisdom of interpretation of dreams from God. The Bible states that God reveals his secrets to his servants. God's communication to his children through dream is understood and interpreted by his spirit and not devil's spirit. You can understand while king Nebuchadnezzar and his magicians toiled woefully to comprehend the series of dreams.

Definition:

Dream: A series of images, ideas, emotions and sensations occurring in the mind during certain stages of sleep (Webster dictionary).

VITAL AND FOUNDATIONAL FACTS ABOUT DREAMS

Dreams from God are inspired and ordained by God for instructions, correcting and how to navigate one's way in this dark world we live in.

Remember the Devil counterfeits every good thing from God. He also instructs and controls his servants through Dreams, but we speak here of Biblical or God inspired dreams! There is a day and night difference between dreams from God and the Devil. There are idle or pizza instilled dreams. There are dreams resulting from over feeding, medication consumption or liquor consumption, which can give you either sweet or drama conglomerated dreams. Read Matt. 17:1-9; I Sam. 28:3-20; I John 4:1.

> "After this, I will pour out my spirit on all kinds of people. Your sons and daughters will prophesy, your old men will dream dreams and your young men will see visions" (Joel 2:28 NIV).

This is also quoted in the New Testament for those who think the Old Testament is outdated. Peter speaks to the religious Jews staying in Jerusalem who were from every country in the world during the day of Pentecost. "God says (not man says): In the last days I will pour out my spirit on all kinds of people. Your sons and daughters will prophesy. Your young men will see visions and your old men will dream dreams" (Acts 2:17, KJV).

The patient man Job, who desperately needed to hear from God, admonishes us thus:

> "For God does speak ~sometimes one way and sometimes another~ even though people may not understand it. He speaks in a dream or a vision of the night when people are in a deep sleep, lying on their beds" (Job 33:14-15 NIV).

Needless to say, he speaks whether in bed, cave, field, or some person's bed or borrowed bed! The key word is the fact that God instructs, directs and shepherds us in Dreams as well as through many other divine processes. Praise God!

THE ROLE OF THE HOLY SPIRIT
IN THE FULFILLMENT OF YOUR DREAM

One of the secondary functions of the Holy Spirit is to give gifts to believers so that we can do his work on Earth. He gives gifts for the perfection-maturity of Saints. The initial work of the Holy Spirit is to draw us to God for Salvation. Other functions include quickening, conviction, teaching, comforting, leading and many more. It will take volumes of Book on its own to do justice to that topic which is not my immediate goal in this Book. For those interested, read John Chapter 6, John Chapter 14, Matthew Chapter 4 and Acts Chapter 2 to begin your study. The Bible teaches that in ancient times, God relayed these messages through the power of the Holy Spirit to His chosen servants by visions and dreams. These messages were also given to the Apostles and the prophets (Amos 5:7, Eph. 3:5).

There are so many references from Holy Scripture, the Bible, where God through dreams communicated with His people. I understand that there are about 121 mentions of dreaming in the Bible and 89 mention of sleep. The first mention of sleep, "Foundation of Dream" occurred with the old man, Adam. I do not intend to get you lost as I almost did during my literature review. You can, however, satisfy your curiosity or for those who desire to take this topic further, read some of these references:

Gen. 20:6: ~ Abimelech was warned not to have an affair with Sarah, Abraham's wife.

Gen. 28:12 ~ Jacob dreamt of a ladder reaching up to heaven, signifying the presence of God as he journeyed to Haran.

It is amazing to know that one third of the Bible relates to visions and dreams. There are important people in the Bible who had their lives monitored and directed by dreams. Some of these characters or respected individuals include Abraham, Joseph, Daniel, Ezekiel, Mary (Jesus Mother), Joseph (Jesus Step Father), Paul formerly called Saul, Cornelius and many others. God as clearly vocalized by Job, always speak to his children. Job really had so many distractions even from his well meaning friends. He had to refocus on God till he heard and followed God's instructions.

The birth of Jesus was revealed in a Dream to some Shepherds in Luke chapter 2:8-15. Dream is a strong source of communication from God; unfortunately we as believers and community of God are losing the gift. We are so bugged up with daily cacophony and distraction that this valuable source of warning and direction is slipping at a jet speed. Someone will ask, what do we do now?

Reconnect by asking according to Matthew 7:7-8 "Ask and God will give to you. Search and you will find. Knock and the door will open for you. Yes, anyone who asks, will receive, everyone who searches will find. And everyone who knocks will have the door opened" (NIV).

I read that one-third of one's live is spent on sleep, the bedrock of dream. We must give significance to that which takes much time of our lives. If sleep without dream refreshes, how much more sleep with dream (communication) from God! It invigorates, excites and gives hope to face our daily struggles. Let us look at this passage together with an open mind. Dreams are sensations (information) occurring in the mind/spirit. Human beings consist of mind (spirit), body and soul.

> I king 3:4-5 read "King Solomon went to Gibeon to offer a sacrifice, because it was the most important place of worship. He offered a thousand burnt offerings on the altar. While he was at Gibeon, the Lord appeared to him in DREAM during the night. God said, "Ask me what-ever you want me to give you".

My God! This is fantastic! Too much! Why did God utilize dreams instead of other means? Dream is between you and God. No middle person who you may think is influencing the message.

Look at this passage, "God is honored for what he keeps secret. Kings are honored for what they can discover" (Proverbs

25:2). You and I are the kings of the Lord, and we must pay attention to our dreams so that we can discover our discoveries. Come on let us go for our discoveries.

"This is true. Bad dreams come from too much worrying, and too many words come from foolish people" (Ecclesiastes 5:3). Well, why not trust God and lean not on your own understanding and let God give you directive and Blessing dreams that will change your life forever?

Your dreams are not junk to be thrown into a basket, rather find out the meaning of your dreams like the Baker and the Butler did. There is a significant message for you from God (Gen. 40:8).

By now you should understand that Dream has its foundation in your maker—God. Get it?

CHAPTER THREE

YOUR FUTURE AND SALVATION ARE REVEALED IN YOUR DREAM

By now I hope you understand my goal that God still speaks or communicates through Dreams for direction, warning, and instructions in righteousness. In no way am I advocating that your life should be focused mainly on dream. The Scripture warns us that many of these forms of communications, vision, Dream, prophecy, etc; may fail as some or other factors come to play but the Agape word (I John 1), the Divine instruction, and the Bible will not fail. God and His word (Rhema—Logos) imbedded in His love will last forever, Amen. There is a dispensation for all things, in all you getting, get understanding and wisdom. God can choose to speak in any form, anyplace, anytime, even through an Ass. We cannot bottle him into anything. He is the, I am that I am. He can show Himself in any color, form, and shape. He is the changer of things yet He is what He is. One thing is sure; He will not violate His word. He is the word and he became flesh to save mankind. Hallelujah

THERE ARE SEVERAL OCCURRENCIES WHERE GOD COMMUNICATED WITH JOSEPH

Let us navigate certain passages in the Bible where God communicated his direction to mankind through Dream.

THE TWO DREAMS OF JOSEPH ARE UNFOLDED (GEN. 37:5-9)

The scripture says it takes two or more witnesses for facts to be established. This is a Known fact in the Bible, and it has been told times without number in churches.

You know how much neglect a thing receives if it is too familiar. We lose the real message behind the sentiment it carries. A preacher titled this passage as "Error of Joseph". Another titled it as "Agony of a Dream" Your Dream or the Dream from God, cannot and will not be in error in your life in the name of Jesus. Amen. God spoke to Joseph directly even as a young boy. Immediately after the second Dream, Joseph knew that God was setting him up for something in the future. Heaven and Earth may pass away but God's word will never pass away. His Father and his brothers knew what the Dream meant, but refused to accept such an usual thing. How can you, the least among the children of Jacob, amount to something superior? We must get two very important facts here. God has chosen Joseph to be the vital wheat, (Bread) for the family. How on Earth can you the least be the vital Bread for the chosen twelve tribes of Jacob? They had Reuben, Judah, and Levi, who should be the real thing, and that could not be you poor frail and 17 (Seventeen) years old boy. Moreover, he was born of the second wife of Jacob. He was relegated to a second class citizen.

Can you see how God chooses the poor, weak and unpopular things of the world to Confound the wise, strong and nobles! God prepared a dream for you when he designed your life. He had you in mind before he planned and put life into you. God has a lesson to show us in this Dream. This is the revelation of Jesus Christ (the Anointed, the Bread of Life); Joseph was a symbol of the coming Messiah, Jesus Christ. In Isaiah chapter 53, we read "who would have believed what we heard?" The brothers refused to believe what they heard. People like to see before they can believe what they hear. The world will see the Glory of God in your life through your dreams, in Jesus name, Amen. The brothers hated, rejected, and Disdained him. They cast him into the pit, sold him to trader, business minded folks, who do not care for human souls but are concerned about the profit they will derive from the transactions. Does not this sound as the treatment inflicted upon Jesus?. They stripped him of his coat of many colors. Does this remind you of Jesus While on the way to the cross?. They lied to the father; may be a lion tore him into Pieces, and this is all we found on the way. God is an awesome God. They said Joseph is dead! But I come to tell you, God lives and his dream, and your dream will never die. What He says, he will do for you. Did you hear me? The visions and dreams he birth in you will come at the appointed time.

God will reveal your future in the dream, but He may not give or reveal all the steps to the actualization. However, he will direct your steps in all you do, and go through as long as you stay TUNE. So stay tuned and focus on your dreams. Your God-given dream will stimulate and keep you connected to your maker. Joseph's Dream kept him from SINS. He had many occasions to be discouraged even when the Baker and the Butler forgot him, but his dream became his source of hope, strength and aspiration. I encourage you to hold on! Hold on to the God of your Dream. Weeping may last for a night but say with me, "Joy comes in the Morning".

THE SECOND DREAM STRENGTHENED JOSEPH

He dreamed again and He told it to his brothers. This infuriated them further and Joseph's father rebuked him. Your Dream is from God; it is not man-made and there is no need for people to get upset with you. The Devil is not worried about your yesterday, some of you are still struggling today; yet the Devil is pretty upset and worried. Have you ever asked yourself why? Joseph had no visible characteristics nor material possession that should infuriate his brothers, yet they did. There must be something not visible/physical to the naked eyes that instigated such anger. Again your yesterday is gone and it is history. The Devil is pretty worried about your TOMORROW! Your dream is surely bright, your star is a super star, and this causes the Devil to panic. God said it a long time ago, and the Devil is aware of this. It is recorded in Genesis 3:15 that the seed of a woman (You and I) will bruise his head as he stays under our feet attempting furiously to hurt our walk with God.

There are three important characters mentioned in this second dream. "Behold the _Sun_ and the _Moon_ and the eleven _Stars_ made obeisance to me (the 12th star). Earlier, I told you that Joseph's life is a protégé of Jesus. God from the beginning, sees the end and designed our lives based upon his blue print. Jesus, the word, has been there with the Father, God right from Genesis. He reveals Jesus all through the scripture by using sample and allegory to showcase him. Go with me to Revelations chapter 12:1, "And there appeared a great wonder in Heaven, a woman clothed with the Sun, and the moon under her feet, and upon her head, is a crown of twelve stars."

Can you see any correlation between the second dream and Revelation of Jesus Christ given to John? This is deep and will take a book to excavate the depth of this Revelation. Suffice at this juncture to say that the Devil has always fought the Church. The Devil is not going to just attack you, he wants to attack your future, your children, your dream, I mean your everything. Glory be to God, He failed in the garden of Eden. He will fail in yours and my life; every attack, arrow and plan to annihilate your dream will be swallowed up. Our testimonies will reign, rule and the trumpet of victory will resound now and forever, Amen.

As every dream of Joseph came to pass, so shall your dream come to fulfillment. God did not prevent trials, but he gave grace to overcome everyone of them. His Faith in God who revealed through Dream kept him from sinning against God. Your faith trust and dependence on the God of revelation for your life will see you through all your trials. Many are the afflictions but God delivers from it all. Joseph was not exempted and the peak of the trial occurred in Potiphar's house.

"After some time the wife of Joseph's master began to desire Joseph, and one day she said to him, come to bed with me. But Joseph refused and said to her, my master trusts me with everything he owns. You are his wife. How can I do such an evil thing? It is a sin against God. "(Gen. 39:7-9). As you read further on to verse 20, you will find that Joseph was lied on and put into prison. Jesus was accused and put on the cross. The interesting remark is that there was God's favor upon his life as he held on to his dream and endured the trials. He looked unto the Hill, the source of his help. It is amazing how God works!

In the book of Genesis chapter 40, we see how God released Joseph from prison by the interpretation of two dreams. The Baker and Butler forgot him until God prepared the way for enthronement. God's time is the best and will not get you into a place where his Grace will not be sufficient. Dreams from God will never fail, and God gives grace, patience, gifts, and favor to see you through. Finally, all God said came to pass and Joseph became, "So to Say" the Bread (Wheat) winner of his family and the Nation where God put him. The parents—symbolized by the Moon and the Sun, and all his brothers (Eleven Stars), bowed before him.

He assured his brothers that they are forgiven; all they meant for evil, God turned his trials and evil treatments around for good. He became the comfort of his father till he died. He reassured his brothers continuously of his love and forgiveness. Is this not similar to what our Lord Jesus is doing for us today? He so loves us that God gave His only begotten Son to die for us. On the cross, He prayed for the abusers and He led captives free and gave us Hope, Love, and Victory. We can now call God our Father, and we continue to renew our hope and dream of fulfillment in our lives.

JOSEPH'S DREAMS WERE USED AS PROTECTIVE AND GUIDING GYRUS

Prophet Isaiah proclaimed the good news between 745 and 680 B.C. during the reign of four Kings of Judah. Isaiah, a well educated, politically astute man had messages for all of Israel, but his ministry was specifically targeted towards Judah the capital of Jerusalem. Unfortunately, he was sawn into pieces by the wicked King Manasseh. He vehemently condemned unholy living but he equally said God will forgive if we forsake our evil ways, through repentance. His messages angered the un-repenting generation and they chose to release "Barnabas" the Malefactor rather than the Holy One of Israel. This background is necessary in order to correlate my topic. Dream will direct, provide ways of escape from evil ones because the Devil is a roaring lion seeking who to devour.

"A child has been born to us; God has given a Son to us. He will be responsible for leading His people. His name will be Wonderful Counselor, Powerful God, Father who lives in Peace. Power and peace will be in His Kingdom and will continue to grow forever. He will rule as King on David's Kingdom. He will make it strong by ruling with justice and goodness from now on and forever. The Lord All-powerful will do this because, of His strong love for His people" (Isaiah 9:6-7), NCV.

Let me highlight some points:

1.   He will lead the people
2.   His name will be Powerful God
3.   He will be a father who lives in peace
4.   His Kingdom will grow forever
5.   He will rule as King on David's Kingdom
6.   He will make the kingdom strong
7.   The Lord All-Powerful will do it

My God! If you were a ruling King in the kingdom of David, what will this mean to you? This seems like a threat and a replacement for the ungodly ruler. You are like Nebuchadnezzar, who has been weighed, and you are out done. You are nothing but a forgotten history. I better get back to my topic before I get lost out of this deep revelation. The wicked King ruling with injustice, no peace, no love, high minded and ambitious king was scared to death. Anyway, to cut the long story short, Jesus finally after about 700 years was born. Remember, the Devil is not panicking because of your yesterday, but because of your future—tomorrow. The reigning Kings, starting from Uzziah, Jotham, Ahaz and Hezekiah, probably panicked all through their Era. The Holy Spirit whispers to me that even the era was sinful, but Hezekiah was a good man because his heart was submissive and he desired God. May you never be associated with company of evil doers in the name of Jesus Christ. Amen. The Sinner runs when no one pursues him. I mean those evil kings feared the future of the promised king. Your tomorrow will be very dangerous to your enemies. Your tomorrow will come whether the Devil likes it or not. I hope you are sounding a loud Amen. Finally, Jesus the fulfilled and promised Messiah came and all the speculations were let lose! Read with me as we navigate to exploit these speculations. Now, Herod is the King of the kingdom of David that we talked about earlier. Here is the core of the matter my dear readers. Now we read that when Joseph thought about these things. What things? A woman that he was engaged to marry has suddenly become pregnant without any sexual contact between them. He called the woman—Mary—and asked her what has happened to her. Mary, with tears rolling down her cheeks, tried to explain her faithfulness. She said "Yes, I have and will always be faithful to you. Neither you nor any person touched me, but something I cannot explain is happening to me. I thought initially that I was sick or some forms of stomach cancer may have invaded my body. But I feel something like human being moving inside me. I feel in-spite of this dilemma, some sort of joy welling up in my soul. I feel God is with me, I feel peace all over me. Hallelujah!"

Note: This woman according to Jewish Law could have been put to death for allegedly committing adultery. "While Joseph thought about these things, an Angel of the Lord came to him in a *dream*. The angel said to Joseph, descendant of David, do not be afraid to take Mary home as your wife, because the baby in her is of the Holy Spirit. She will give birth to a son, and you will name him Jesus because he will save his people from their sins" (Matthew 1:20-21).

If God used Dream to communicate to Joseph in such a time of decision, a crucial time when the Savior of the world was involved, at such a period of apparent embarrassment to the Virgin Mary, how much more do you and I need to hear from God through such means? Do not underrate our God's given Dream; it is a vital source of divine direction. It is very much needed in your journey here on Earth.

THE WISE MEN WENT TO SEARCH FOR THE NEW BORN

The wise men went to search for the new born King-Jesus. Sure enough, they found him with Mary and Joseph and did what they needed to do. They bowed down and worshipped him. Moreover, they opened their bags and gave him treasures of gold, frankincense, and myrrh.

> "But God warned the wise men in a Dream not to go back to Herod, so they returned to their country by a different way. Dream from God is a sure clear directive instrument that is inevitable in our modern day as it was before. "Jesus Christ is the same yesterday, today and forever" (Heb. 13:8).

> "After they left, an Angel of the Lord came to Joseph in a Dream and said "Get Up! Take the child and his mother and escape to Egypt, because Herod is looking for the child so that he can kill him; Stay in Egypt until I tell you to return" (Matt. 2:13).

Sure enough verses 16-18 record the salvage and massive destruction of male babies, who were two years old or younger, in Bethlehem and the surrounding area.

DREAMS DIRECT, GUIDE
AND PROTECT THE DREAMER

Let me conclude this chapter with yet another scenario, showing that God communicates through Dream.

After Herod died, an Angel of the Lord spoke to Joseph in a dream while he was in Egypt. The Angel said "Get Up! Take the child and his mother and go to the Land of Israel, because the people who were trying to kill the child are now dead" (Matthew 2:20) NIV.

Your time has come when all you seek to kill you, kill your dream, and your success, will be exterminated because they refused to leave you alone. They vowed not to rest until you, your family are relegated and replaced. God hears their wishful desires, and God himself will return all their evil plans upon them. I say God will return all evils against you, the Balak curses against you to the senders in Jesus name, Amen.

There are enemies that will fear God, repent and cease from their wicked ways. To such, God promised they will be forgiven, but those like the Ethiopian Leopard that their skins can never change, I say they will perish in Jesus Name. They have troubled you enough and they cannot continue their nefarious activities on you or any other person. There may be some of you who wish to tolerate your destroyers, but I refuse to let those things God has chosen to destroy, to linger around me, Amen.

Joseph went to Isreal with the child and his mother. But when Joseph heard that Archelaus was now the king in Judea because his father, Herod, had died, he (Joseph) was afraid to go there. After being warned in a dream, he went to the area of Galilee (Matt. 2:21-22).KJV

I will be doing a big injustice if I do not emphatically emphasize the needed ingredient for dream come true. You must obey quickly when you hear (whichever form) from God. This communication could be through Vision, Rhema, Epistle, or Dream. Obedience is better than sacrifice. Those who do not obey God as the Holy Spirit ministers will soon be on their own.

CHAPTER FOUR

DREAMS PROVIDE NEEDED CLUES FOR CRUCIAL DECISIONS

Herod and the other kings, rulers and religious zealots misunderstood the cause of Jesus. Even the Disciples had their portions of misunderstanding. In many cases, he will say to his Disciples "how long will I be with you, and how long will I teach you this fact, Oh ye of little faith". Moreover, he will say, "who do you think the son of man is"? I have been with you so long and yet you do not know who I am. The audience and the Disciples will say, "Show us the father". There is a particular incidence that deserves looking at as recorded in the book of Matthew.

A mother asks Jesus a favor. This was the mother of two of Jesus disciples—Zebedee's wife. She came, bowed before him and asked for a favor. At this point, Jesus asked what she wanted. She wanted Jesus to promise her that both of her two sons (among the twelve disciples) will each sit one on his right and the other on his left side in his kingdom. In other word, let my two boys be your adjutants, direct assistants, key guys, your men that would be recognized through whom others can reach you. Put them in powerful positions in your kingdom that I see coming soon. I want to be the mother of those in authority, people to reckon with in your peaceful kingdom. I see it very soon Jesus, It is coming! Jesus may have just told the twelve disciples that a change is about to happen. In three days, the temple will be torn down in three days, and I will rebuild it in three days. Men, I tell you, everybody is getting excited.

Jesus in his wisdom quickly asked the sweet mother, "can you drink the cup that I am about to drink?" The two disciples standing with their mother quickly jumped in. They have been quietly saying Amen to their mother's compelling request. Now, this is their opportunity to show that they are not wimps. Yes, we can firmly stand the test of time. I bet you they did not really understand what Jesus was talking about at all. Jesus was full of thoughts and this is not the time to argue but give the answer straight away. I can see the mother getting excited too. She is mussing, "Oh boy, my boys are tough and Jesus will be convinced of their love, strength and the stuff they possess." Hear what Jesus said, "You will drink from my cup" Men, the boys are saying, "Yes, he got us!" "But I cannot choose who will sit at my right hand or my left. Those places belong to those for whom my father has prepared them (Matthew 20:23).

When the other ten disciples heard this, they were furious with the two. The mother quietly took to her heal and probably wondering if she has gotten her children into some sort of mess. I can imagine someone like Peter and Andrew his brother being the first two called wanting to start a fight. Peter was kind of short tempered and was somewhat muscular, and getting ready to unload upon those boys if they do not stop the mess. I guess mother Zebedee gently gave a blink of eye to her sons and took a humble departure and left Master Jesus to handle his boys.

Jesus took the occasion to teach them humility, self service, and what he came to do, which is to be ransom for many people.

JESUS WAS ACCUSED BEFORE PONTIUS PILATE

Dream played a vital role when Jesus was brought before Pontius Pilate.

Pontius Pilate was the governor at the time of the arrest of Jesus Christ and false witnesses mounted up against him. Jesus stood before Pilate the governor and Pilate knew Jesus was being falsely accused, but he was careful not to offend the general populace. Politicians are the same, no matter the continent, Country, Western world, European, African or Asian world. They dance to the tune of the people—evil or good! There are a few exceptions not to generalize my opinion. He questioned Jesus carefully and logically finding ways for prove Jesus' innocence. But Jesus was not going to stop drinking the cup that has been prepared for him. Isaiah 53 has declared what awaits him at this time. "He was wounded for the wrong we did, crushed for the evil we did, He was bitten down but he did not say a word for his defense. He was like a lamb being led to be killed. Men took him away roughly and unfairly but by his stripes we were healed".

So Pilate said to Jesus, "Don't you hear them accusing you of all these things?" But Jesus said nothing in answer to Pilate, and Pilate was very surprised at this" (Matthew 27:13-14) NIV.

PILATE'S WIFE HAD A WARNING DREAM FROM GOD

The Power of Dream affected the reaction of Pilate's wife.

While Pilate was sitting there on the judge's seat, his wife sent a message to him: "Don't do anything to that man, because he is innocent. Today, I had a dream about him, and it troubled me very much" (Matt. 27:19 KJV) NIV.

Dream is a universal way God talks to his creation. Like a conscience, given to all flesh irrespective of your race, color, sex, or religious background. As long as you are created by God, he will communicate with you. Prophecy, Vision, Logos, etc, may be selective, but Dream is not limited. It is a universal communication system of the mind between human beings and their God, their maker consequently; it is very essential we learn to pay attention and seek to understand what God is saying.

GOD SPOKE TO KING NEBUCHADNEZZAR THROUGH A DREAM

***In this King Nebuchanezzar had a frightful dream.

There was a prophet who prophesied during the reign of this popular king. God gave Daniel the gift of interpretation of dreams in addition to the gift of prophecy. Daniel himself received messages through revelation, dream and vision too. He was blessed of the Lord! God needed to speak with Nebuchadnezzar as a ruler of his people. The Israelites, though stubborn, always gripping, complaining and disobedient, like us, before you jump into wrong conclusion, we, today, are not different; we are chosen generation, born again and filled with the Holy Spirit but during trials, we act, talk and ponder terrible things as if we are not the same who shout Hallelujah on Sunday or during church services. We easily forget where God has brought us from and through. We allow fear to dominate our lives, wonder if God is the same yesterday, today and forever. We forget yesterday, we forget those red seas, those Jericho walls, those Lions den, those attacks, those radical write offs, those deserts where God prepared tables (not one) and lastly, those no-ways that God made to be ways. God will never forsake his elects though we mess up times without number. The prodigal son will always find favor, rest and forgiveness as long as he returns home. God spoke to Nebuchadnezzar, ruler of the people in a dream.

"During Nebuchadnezzar's second year as a king, he had dreams that bothered him and kept him awake at night" (Daniel 2:1).

He sought for the magicians, wizards, fortune-tellers and his wise men but none could give him the answer to those dreams. It was made harder because he completely forgot the dreams. I will discuss this scene in this book because this is the strategy God used to favor his faithful servant Daniel.

Death was pronounced upon ALL SEERS, and this would include Daniel, Hananiah, Mishael, and Azariah. Daniel asked his friends to pray that the God of Heaven would show them mercy and help them understand this secret so that they (he and his friends) would not be killed with the other wise men of Babylon.

During the night, God had mercy and he through a vision explained the secret of the Dream to Daniel. As a result, the dreams were revealed and explained. The word says in II Chronicle 7:14, I paraphrase that "If God's people will humble themselves in prayer, repent and turn from their wicked ways, he will hear their prayers, heal their land (lives) and do a great thing in their lives". God has not and will not change. He is the changer that does not change. His mercy endures forever. Faithful is he that called us.

THE ANXIETY OF A KING WHO
FORGOT HIS DREAM

This is a very unusual situation but it is designed so to confound the supposedly wise seers who worked by the evil spirit. I say power pass power. Like the scene of Moses before pharaoh, the snakes of Moses consumed those of the magicians. God made the situation very tough for the king and his seers to reveal the glory and the gift that he imputed into Daniel. God uses tough and difficult situations today to reveal His Grace in His chosen and faithful children. Bad economic times afford opportunity for God's servants to prosper.

Read I kings chapter 17, famine was an open door for Elijah to change the life of the Zarephath widow. The falling axe provided opportunity for Elijah's miraculous acts. The death of the only son of the widow in Luke 7: 11-15, and the death of Lazarus (John 11) proved that God can raise the dead even in a stinking state. Both Lazarus and this man have been embalmed before the Lord arrived.

May difficult stances in your life be opportunities for Miracles, breakthrough, and great things for you, in Jesus name, Amen! God is All-wise and he will not take you where his Grace does not abound.

CHAPTER FIVE

LOOKING AT HINDRANCES, TRIALS, AND TEMPTATIONS IN THE LIFE OF A CHOSEN VESSEL

Your God given dream will definitely affect your life; as I earlier said, your walk, talk and activities will be modified. It is like Apostle Paul said in second Corinthians 5:17 that if anyone belongs to Christ, he is a new creation. The old things have gone; everything is made new!

Joseph's dreams affected his life to the magnitude of watching his behavior—he refused to be affected negatively by his environment. He applied the principle of godliness. He did not let bitterness, anger, and disappointment cloud his faith. He looked unto the Hill from where comes his help. Apostle Peter in his first Epistle gives encouragement for suffering Christians. During your trials and tribulations, God's power protects you through your faith until way of escape or God's interventions come.

This assurance of God's intervention, the Hope on the way keeps you happy though now for a short time various and different kinds of troubles may make you sad. Remember Peter exhorts that these troubles come to prove that your faith is pure. The purity of faith is worth more than gold, which can be proved to be pure by fire but will ruin. Your ability to endure trials will at the end bring great Glory to God. The Lord will say welcome my beloved son or daughter in whom I am so proud. In our trials God is there with us, but you can only see through the eyes of faith. Without this kind of faith, you cannot please God, and you may actually be frustrated and give up. The Devil is after your dream which is the revelation and assurance of your tomorrow.

Again using the life of Joseph we find out how his dream got him into a big mess. Some people who know, see and hear your tomorrow revealed through your dream, will do all they can to hinder it. They will talk about you, laugh you to scorn, tease your dream and even say you are crazy. Jesus was called to a home where a young girl was dying. There was a slight delay because of others who needed his touch and healing. God in his infinite wisdom allowed the delay to prove his resurrection power. Jesus told the family not to fear that the young girl was sleeping; Even those who were around, weeping and fainting just burst into a loud laughter. What a joker they have invited to this place! The scripture says Jesus expelled the faithless out but proceeded with only the faithful. We must let faith expel fears and doubt and hold on to the horn of our salvation. What God says, and reveals he will do in Jesus name, Amen.

Joseph was hated by those (brothers) who heard his dreams. This was the first trial that shocked him.

"When Joseph's brothers saw their father loved Joseph more than he loved them, they hated their brother and could not speak to him politely. One time Joseph had a dream, and when he told his brothers about it, they hated him even more" (Gen. 37:4-5) NIV.

Here comes another one. Joseph's brothers saw him coming from far away. Before he reached them, they made a plot to kill him. They said to each other, here come the *dreamer*. "Let's kill him and throw his body into one of the wells. We can tell our father that a wild animal killed him, then we will see what will become of his dreams" (Gen.37:18-20) NIV.

They took him out of the dry pit and sold him to the Ishmaelites for eight ounces of silver. That was cheap indeed for a human being. The blood of goat was substituted for Joseph's. He was later sold to Potiphar, an officer to the king of Egypt and Captain of the palace guard.

There were several trials not recorded that he put up with, but he kept looking forward to his dreams.

POTIPHAR'S WIFE FALSELY ACCUSED JOSEPH

After some time, Potiphar's wife began to desire Joseph, and one day she asked Joseph to have sexual relations with him.

Joseph refused to succumb to the temptation; consequently, he was lied upon and put into the deepest, more secured part of the prison. That is what we call today maximum security cell. I wonder how much of your faith has been tested and you still remain unshakable. We never heard he was complaining to the other fellow prisoners. He kept his faith on the God of his dream. I do not intend to say he did not feel bad, and I believe the Devil bombarded him with thoughts. May be he pondered if God has forgotten, and if those dreams will ever see the day light. The situation frankly looked bleak and there appeared to be no way at all. If you were in his place your goal probably will be to be set free from prison. Come to think of it, what is the need of getting out of prison? Many people in prison for very long years prefer to stay in there than coming out into a horrifying, unfriendly and frustrating environment. Freedom becomes fearful and you try to adjust to a changed environment. You lose your right to vote and you are labeled, and your name gets pulled out of every computer whenever your social security is entered into the computerized system.

In Joseph's case, remember that he was now in a strange country where there was no father. Benjamin, his younger brother was left to face his cruel siblings and a lamenting father who refused to be consoled. He was constantly facing the coat stained with blood, not of another human being, but of a goat or another animal. Goats are not too wise—just dumb.

THOSE YOU HELP MAY FORGET YOU

One of the gifts he had was ability to interpret dream. He was blessed with dreams and their interpretations. He could have chosen to hide or ignore the gifts of Help to interpret dreams while in prison. There was tendency for him to feel abandoned or forgotten. This was enough for frustration, bitterness and real bad feeling. He kept his cool and kept loving and willing to relieve the pains of others. There were two kings officers—the Butler and Baker—who were also kept in the same prison. It is encouraging that God's grace and favor were always with Joseph wherever trials took him. God's dream for your life will usher favor, direction, and grace upon you. Amen.

Most times we allow the trials to overwhelm us that we hardly see God's provisions in our lives. The captain of the guard put the two prisoners (Butler and Baker) in Joseph's care and they stayed there with Joseph. Apparently, Joseph had stayed there for a long enough time to earn him the trust. As a result he was given charge over the captain's offenders.

One night, the Baker and the Butler in the same prison had some dreams. Each had his own dream but did not know the meaning. Joseph observed these anxious and frustrated individuals and asked why they looked unhappy that day. How could someone be in a prison and you ask why is he unhappy? Is prison a place of merriment? There are, I guess, classes of unhappiness, there is the one that is deeper than face expression. The one that affects the soul cannot be covered with fake smile. We are in a world where no man's sorrow is another man's. However, this was not the attitude of Joseph. He was always willing to help when he could and his light shone before men (irrespective of the environment) so that God could be glorified.

The two officers told Brother Joseph their predicament. "We both had dreams last night, but no one is able to explain their meanings to us" (Gen. 40:8) NIV.

God has the answer to your predicament or dilemma. Joseph assured them that God is the only one who can explain the meaning of dreams. God is good. Joseph gave the glory, accolade and accreditation to God. Humility and trust in God is here exemplified. The dreams were explained to both the Butler and the Baker. Joseph made a simple request to the Butler-remember me, be kind to me and tell the king about me.

Surely after three days as the dream entailed, the Butler was restored to the original position while the Baker was hanged on a pole.

What is then the trial? You may ask. The Butler forgot Joseph in the prison. He did not even mention his name to the king. He did not, but what man intends for evil God uses to bring the best result for his chosen children. The time when it is right, God himself will bring it to pass with the biggest miracle in Jesus name, Amen.

These are some of the trials that Joseph faced in his days.

Your dreams must face trials, but remember the bigger your dreams, the bigger the size of your trials and tribulations; similarly, the bigger and better the result.

YOU HAVE A ROLE IN FULFILLING YOUR DREAM

☐⇨ Stay focus on your Dream

☐⇨ Let your dream motivate you to stay away from sins

☐⇨ Be determined that he who has begun a good work in you will complete it (Phil. 1:6; Rom. 8:28; Rom. 8:18)

☐⇨ Be humble even as Christ humbled himself (Phil. 2:5-11)

☐⇨ Have a loving/forgiving Heart (Gen. 45:1-15)

☐⇨ Give God praise continuously (Ps. 103; Acts 16:25)

☐⇨ Pray in the Holy Spirit and Meditate upon God's words (Ps.119: 105).

CHAPTER SIX

The Leadership And Provision Of God In The Fulfillment Of Your Dream

(A) GOD'S FAVOR IS AVAILABLE UPON YOUR LIFE

God never gives a vision or dream without the provision or guidance to fulfilling the assignments. God has a unique methodology of setting us up for his blessing and direction. When he called Moses, he gave him a vision of the burning flames, and equally told him that Aaron would be glad to accompany him and be his spoke's man. He equally supernaturally changed his Rod to be whatsoever God desires it to be. The Lord himself is the, I AM that I AM, he also blesses with something that would make us unique to accomplish tasks needed.

In the case of Joseph, favor became his apparel wherever he went. His brothers stripped him off his coat of many colors but God gave him unseen covering or coat of favor that man cannot strip from him.

"The Lord was with Joseph, and he became a successful man" Gen. 39:2. A slave we are told became successful in everything he did. That takes a special favor from God. He was so trusted that he was a blessing to the household of Portiphar.

The Lord blessed everything (not some, but all) that belonged to his master—both internal and external businesses. You better believe that this is God's favor. This is similar to Abraham who was tremendously favored by God. God even said that he would bless those who bless him, curse those who curse him, and make him a great Nation. Moreover, all the people of the earth will be blessed through him. This is awesome! Your dream must be enveloped with obedience, humility, and patience. Another big favor that catapulted him to his destination came when he interpreted the king's dreams.

(B) GIFT OF INTERPRETATION IS AVAILABLE

God deals with individuals according to his perfect plan he has for the individuals. If God blesses you with a car, don't you believe he can also give you the ability to get a drivers license?

In some cases the dreamer may not be able to interpret the dream but if this is from God, he will lead you to a person who will interpret it for you. Paul had a vision on the Damascus road and God sent Ananias to help him out with direction and proper analysis of the revelation. In the case of Joseph, he was equally blessed with the gift of interpretations of dreams.

The scripture in proverbs states that a man's gift will make room for him, and bring him before great people.

Joseph, along with his God given dream, was blessed with a unique gift to take him to his destination. God, who expects us to play our role, does his part too. His gift of interpretation landed him to the right throne of grace. That is the provision and the leadership of God!

The King's Dream was surely Interpreted

The King said to Joseph, "I have had a dream, but no one can explain its meaning to me, I have heard that you can explain a dream when someone tells it to you" (Gen. 41:15) NIV.

Listen to the response of Joseph. He responded "I am not able to explain meanings of dreams, but God will do this for the king" (Gen. 41:16) NIV. All ministers of the Gospel should learn from the humility of this man. Those who God has given a dream of greatness must learn to be humble and give God and God alone the Glory! He who must exercise authority must learn to be subject to authority. Pride, God hates, has caused many to lose their crowns. The king told Joseph his dreams and Joseph being led of God, explained in detail what God was revealing to the king.

(C) GOD GIVES THE GIFT OF KNOWLEDGE

Meticulously, Joseph through the gift of knowledge explained to the king that both dreams meant the same thing.

God was revealing to the king that there will be seven years of plenty followed by seven years of hunger. The last seven years will be so severe that the people will forget that the initial seven years of plenty ever existed. This was going to be a horrifying and terrible famine that will affect the whole earth.

(D) APOSTLE JAMES REMINDS US THAT GOD GIVES WISDOM TO ANY ONE WHO ASKS

"So let the king choose a man who is very wise and understanding and set him over the land of Egypt. Let the king also appoint officers over the Land, who should take one-fifth of all the food that is grown during the seven good years. They should gather all the food that is produced during the good years that are coming, and under the king's authority they should store the grain in the cities and guard it. By this the people in Egypt will not die during the seven years of hunger" (Gen.41:33-36) NIV.

YOUR DREAMS WILL COME TRUE

God, the *Giver* of your dream will fulfill the dreams at His appointed time. Weeping may endure for the night but joy comes in the morning. All our trials and tribulations prepare us for the dream. Habakkuk says though it tarries but, it will surely come to pass. Hallelujah. Divine and supernatural interventions are on the way to fulfill your dream. Do not give up but be steadfast, un-moveable and trust God till it happens. The closer the fulfillment, the more stones, darts and doubts the Devil will try to bring. The butterfly in its maggot (almost complete) stage looks uglier, but its redemption is closest. The Butler forgot Joseph but God did not. The king himself sought for Joseph, and he received a dignified reception to the dignified position. He did not beg to see the king, did not ask for appointment through the king's secretary and adjutants, but God made a way where there seemed to be no way. Joseph became Governor over Egypt, and he was responsible for selling grains to people who came to buy.

THERE ARE STAGES OF
THE MANIFESTATION OF YOUR DREAM

1. Jacob learned that these was grain in Egypt during the terrible famine (Gen. 42:6)
2. The brothers said "No my master, we come as your servants just to buy food" (Gen. 42:10)
3. The brothers of Joseph bowed down to the ground in front of him(Joseph)
4. When they returned the second time to Egypt to buy food (Gen. 43:26)

The brothers kept bowing down before Joseph as the first dream predicted. Through all trials, Joseph used all that God has taught him to the fulfillment of God's purpose for his life.

Joseph knew his brothers all along, but they did not recognize him. It is amazing how God works, his wonders to perform. His brothers were blind folded by God. They remembered the evil they did to their brother who they thought they will never see again.

Finally, Joseph revealed himself to his brethren because he could not hide or control his emotion any longer.

He dismissed his servants and said to his brothers "I am Joseph. Is my father alive?" His brothers were very afraid, but he drew them closer and spoke to them kindly. He told them he was not any Joseph but Joseph their brother whom they had sold as a slave to the Midianites. It is incredible how he comforted his brothers, "God sent me here ahead of you to save your lives and that of the other people". God sent him, he declared, ahead of you to make sure that you have some descendants left on Earth and to keep you alive in an amazing way. He said "It was not you who sent me here but God" (Gen.45:8). Isn't this similar to the attitude of Jesus even while on the cross? He requested that God will forgive those who were crucifying him. God allowed Jesus to suffer and die a cruel death on the cross to save mankind.

The resurrection and His shed blood on the cross bring salvation to all who receives him, whom he called not my servants but brethren. Joseph displayed such a forgiving spirit that we who call upon God today need to emulate.

JACOB WENT TO EGYPT AS DIRECTED BY DREAM

It was a great river of joy that flooded the soul of Jacob as he met his son Joseph!

He that was declared once dead is alive today. He is not only living in the land of the abundance, but God has made him the highest officer of the king of Egypt. My God!

When Jacob heard the good news—I call this the best news of his entire life-he took all he had and started on his trip. Before going to Egypt, he went to Beersheba and he offered sacrifices to the God of his father Isaac, the son of Papa Abraham, the man who obeyed God. This is the man who walked by faith and not by sight; the man who did not waiver, but focused on his God given *dream*. This is the man whose eyes, visions, did not dim. This is the man who saw beyond the deadness of his body and his wife's body but trusted in the God who spoke. My God!

Jacob offered sacrifices to God. He was not too excited to forget to give God the Glory like many of us would have done. He was like the only one leper among those healed and returned to give God the praise while the other nine (ungrateful) went on to party. He believed though he has not spoken to or seen his Joseph in his fulfilled destiny. He gave thanks and sacrifices to God. During the night in a vision, (Dream's sister), God called upon Jacob, "Jacob, Jacob" He answered, "Here I am". God said, "I am God, the God of your father. Don't be afraid to go to Egypt because I will make your descendants a great Nation there. I will go to Egypt with you, and I will bring you out of Egypt again" (Gen. 46:2-4) KJV.

THE LAND OF GOSHEN REPRESENTS DREAM COME TRUE

The Land of Goshen offered a wonderful place for the family of Jacob.

Jesus said "Don't let your heart be troubled. Trust in God, and trust in me. There are many rooms in my father's house; I will not tell you this if it were not true. I am going there to prepare a place for you" (John14:1-2) NIV.

GOSHEN IS YOUR DESTINATION

This was a perfect place where Joseph's brethren and Dad reared their Animals without discrimination and conflict between them and the Egyptians.

Jacob told the king of Egypt that he has been wondering from place to place. "It has been short but filled with trouble, only one hundred thirty years. My ancestors lived much longer than I." (Gen.47:9) NIV.

A summary of life on earth: A man born of a woman is full of troubles. King Solomon in his book of Ecclesiastes gives vivid description of activities of and in life. This book is worth studying and applying to life today. It will blow your mind and make you think twice. Earthly goals, apart from God will not bring us happiness. Jacob remembered the headache suffered in the hands of his ten children; yet he lived and prayed for them. Money, fame and accomplishments will not bring lasting happiness. A life totally submissive and devoted to God will bring happiness. A youthful life obedient to God brings Joy at the end. Vision and your God given dream keep hope going and Hope renews your life. Oh, how old man Jacob viewed his days on Earth!

Thank God for Goshen. A place of *Dreams* fulfilled; A place where tears are wiped off; A place of forgiveness; A place where all the enemies plans failed; A place where bitterness has no root; A place where God's fulfillment is glorified and where you can say finally, Thank God. It has been a long, rough, trying long journey; But God . . . .

Jacob finally blessed and adopted the offspring of Joseph. That is what God will do for all who come through Jesus Christ our redeemer.

Jacob adopted Manasseh and Ephraim as his own sons. I hear someone singing a song "Double, Double". In the place of Joseph thought to have died but now returned, God doubled his number of children. In Jacob's own statement he said, "your two sons, who were born here in Egypt before I came, will be counted as my own sons. Ephraim and Manasseh will be my sons just as Reuben and Simeon are my sons" (Gen. 48:5). "But ye received the spirit of adoption, whereby we cry, Abba, Father" (Romans 8:15b) KJV. As adopted children of God, we have great benefits. "So God is able, always, to save those who come to God through Jesus because he always lives, asking God to help us" (Heb. 7:25) NIV.

The suffering, death and resurrection of Jesus brought many to God for salvation.

Consequently, we can now say the following:

1. We are blessed and highly favored (Eph.1:3)
2. We are anointed to prosper (I John 2:20)
3. We are redeemed from sin, sickness and poverty (Gal.3:13)
4. We are justified, Sanctified and victorious (Rom. 5:1, I Thess. 5:23, I Cor.15:57)
5. We are righteous, kings and beloved (II Cor. 5:21, Rev. 1:6, I John 3:2)

6. We are saints and the body of Christ (Eph. 2:19; Eph. 4:16)
7. We are fruitful trees, and God's kingdom workmanship (John 15:8; Eph. 2:10)
8. We are citizens of God's kingdom and Ambassador for Christ
9. (Eph. 2:19; II Cor. 5:20)

CHAPTER SEVEN

GOD AND HIS
WORD ARE ONE

So far, I have tried to familiarize you with various ways God speaks to his people. I have mentioned and cited incidences in the Bible to illustrate my points. I explained some and mentioned several ways—Divine revelation, revelation through the Holy Spirit, Christ Revelation as in Book of Revelation, Fuller Revelation, Rhema, Logos, Trial of faith, Audible Voice, Personal Appearance, Act of God and *Dream*.

I can not say that I have covered all means through which God speaks to his people and the world. You as a child of God must trust and identify means of hearing from God by utilizing all the means God has blessed you with. Remember some of the means are not always easy to comprehend. Evangelist Phillip was directed to the Ethiopian Eunuch who was reading the Book of Esaias. Phillip asked if he understood what he was reading, and he said, "how can I understand when there is no one to explain it and guide me" (Acts 8:26-31).

There are some Visions, revelations, Rhema and the scriptures that are straight forward. On the other hand, there are many Dreams that need interpretation. Joseph, our main character, had the two dreams that were clear even the brothers and daddy Jacob knew the meaning of the Dreams. There are people God has given the gift of interpretation, and they will gladly help you without charging you. We don't sell gifts of God; we see this as Joseph interpreted the dreams of the Butler and the Baker. My Late Papa, Apostle Dr. Samuel Ogbonmwan had numerous gifts, and he used them freely to bless God's people.

We must however remember that God cannot be boxed in; He can do all things and speak through any means He chooses. I warn that no one should run after visions, dreams, and prophecies, but our Lord Jesus Christ, the Giver of gifts. Gifts help us appreciate God; they guide and instruct us if discreetly utilized. Above all the Holy Spirit of God is there to help us know the truth.

I WISH TO OFFER MY CONCLUDING STATEMENTS

In conclusion, I have prayerfully discussed some areas that may be familiar or otherwise. I strongly believe that God is the same yesterday, today and forever.

He communicated in the past through various ways particularly through dreams, and it is essential today to re-awake this gift of *Dreams* and to pray for understanding, wisdom and knowledge.

The scripture in Hosea states that God's people perish for lack of knowledge, (Hos. 4:6). I paraphrased this quotation.

Again, many faithful and God fearing leaders and Apostles were led by true *dreams* from God. They sought understanding of their dreams, and God helped them to govern, direct, instruct and improve the qualities of the lives of the people they led. Needless to say again and again, that we must test every Spirit (I John 4: 1-3).

The Devil tries to counterfeit every good work of God. The Devil does give dreams to people; there is however, a litmus test to differentiate between them.

Every dream, vision, revelation or any form of communication that contradicts the word of God is not of God. God's word reveals God's mind, and God and his word are the same. I hope those who had an open mind as they read this book, may have gained something. You may have been challenged, re-affirmed your dreams or have seen a need to re-awake your God given gifts. Your gifts are your tools to improve your life and of those people God brings to your life.

There are many sermons about Devil's dream, but my goal is to focus on the power of our dreams. Jesus has given us Victory, and we are more than conquerors through Christ that strengthens us. God has not given us the spirit of fear but of a sound mind. When Satan brings any of his dreams, pray immediately and cancel his plans in the name of Jesus.

Joseph's gifts made room for him because he was dedicated, faithful and humble to realize the values and purposes for his gifts. God blesses us to bless others and freely you were given and freely you shall utilize the gift.

The bottom line is to glorify God. God Bless you. This is my prayer.

This author has written some other books that will bless your soul and they are:

1)   Vision Without People Perish
2)   Seven Reasons for Giving to God
3)   Bitterness, a Cancer in the Church
4)   God's Simple Tips for Ministers
5)   You Can Make It—The Ogbonmwan Way
6)   The Glorious Exit of the Man
7)   Workers Manual for CACGM
8)   CD's and DVD's

For a complete list and order information Email mogbonmwan@yahoo.com, Providenceplus@yahoo.com or write: P. O. BOX 87126 Houston, TX 77287

Visit CACGM worldwide.org

About The Author

Rev. Dr. Matthew Ogbonmwan, Senior Pastor of Christ Apostolic Church of God Mission Houston branch, Associate Pastor CACGM Headquarter in Benin City, Foreign Mission Superintendent and Grand Patron of Great Partner Network, lives in Houston Texas United States of America with his wife Rev. Bernel and family.

As the Foreign Mission Superintendent of Christ Apostolic Church of God Mission, he has pioneered the establishment of many branches of Christ Apostolic Church of God Mission in several countries all over the globe to God's glory. Taking his experiences, skills, knowledge and his mentor's and father's (Apostle Dr. S. E Ogbonmwan founder of CACGM World-Wide, of blessed memory) tutoring, he has written several books. Some of his ministerial works include, books, DVDs, CDs. He travels extensively.

Across the globe preaching, teaching, organizing conferences, conventions and crusades making all efforts to equip the workers of God for the world's final harvest (Matthew 28 verses 19-20).

Some of his books include the following: Vision without people perish, Seven reasons for giving to God, Bitterness a cancer in the Church, Spiritual Nuggets to the Young Ministers, God's simple Tips for Ministers, You can make it, The glorious exit of the Man, Christian—Workers Training/Manual, and this particular one-the Dream. He has featured in many Television programs and had his program, Hour of Faith, on the first Christian Television in Houston Texas founded by Elder Thomas now owned by Jones and Marcus—"Celebration center".

CAST FOR THE BOOK "DREAM"

Every child of God is born with a designed blue print for his or her life. Many spend their life time attempting to discover that particularly designed life blue print for navigating and succeeding in life.

Some people discover the blue print half way along their life span, and once discovered they start the building plan for their life. They may finally succeed with much and tougher endeavor before death do them part. A good example of this was Apostle Paul on his Damascus road. He spent major part of his life breathing out threatening and slaughter against the disciples of the Lord whom he finally defended and became apologetic all his life time. He was able to propagate the Gospel of Jesus through his preaching, teaching, and literature than any of the Disciples as recorded in the New Testament.

On the other hand, some go through their lifetime groping and getting frustrated with life and wondering where they missed it in life. As a result of their frustration, they get into habits, practices and such activities like Jacob's in the bible, who stole his brother's birth rite and Simon, who offered money to the apostles to acquire power that will enable him lay hands on people to receive the Holy Ghost.

The third Class of people who are blessed in their early age received the blue print, fully or partially, that guided them in their life journey. A very good example of an individual in this category is my main character Joseph in this book.

The revelation of God's plan (I call it blue print) aided him to be focus, determined, kept him from horrendous sins, and aided him to keep his mind on God. In many circumstances that would cause many to lose faith, trust and dependence on their God; however, Joseph believed that he, who has begun a good work in his life will bring it to a successful end. When the Butler forgot him in Jail, he did not become bitter but trusted he who has spoken and who will perform his words.

This book is not about interpretations of dream, vision nor other forms through which God communicates, but it is to challenge you to seek your God given life blue print for you. It is not anything to dis-regard nor be ignorant about. The Lord said" my people perish for lack of knowledge" God does not make without a purpose and his purpose for one's life is the blue print we must seek in our lives. Jesus himself said his meat is to do the work of his father, God. The scripture further emphasizes this by saying" for this purpose the son of man is manifested".

Modeica reminded Queen Esther to seek God's blue print for her life; perhaps it is for this purpose God raised you Esther, an orphan and a foreigner, to be chosen as the wife of the King